To:,
Adrianne
Become
Wine
Chic

Wine Chic Women

Wine Chic Women

A Wine Image Makeover

Jolie Mouton and Lisa Traiser

iUniverse, Inc.

New York Lincoln Shanghai

Wine Chic Women
A Wine Image Makeover

iUniverse, Inc.

For information address:
iUniverse, Inc.
2021 Pine Lake Road, Suite 100
Lincoln, NE 68512
www.iuniverse.com

ISBN: 0-595-30289-0

Printed in the United States of America

Think of wines like girlfriends; each one has a different body style and mood.

Dedicated to all women who have a passion and dream. Follow them.

Preface

We have a passion for wine. When you've found your love, it's like body surfing; a huge wave fills your soul with inner happiness, chartering you into even bigger and deeper waters. Sometimes you master it perfectly, hopping the wave, letting it skim you all the way to shore. The adrenaline flows, and you rush back in for more. Other times, this emotion can lead you into dark, dangerous waters, slamming you into the rocky shore line, piercing your delicate skin. True passion, however, pops you back up like a buoy, anchoring you there until you're ready for more.

Our journey together, which ultimately led to this book, began while we were negotiating over a case of wine. (Lisa is a former wine shop owner—now that's true love!) Our common interest in wine drifted us into a beautiful bay of water called friendship. We began to exchange endless stories of wine country trips, experiences (some quite embarrassing), entertaining dilemmas, and wine and food creations. Realizing we had waves of wine knowledge between the two of us (over 18 years combined), we decided to toss around the idea of translating these experiences and knowledge into book form. We wanted not only to find a way to share our wine experiences, dilemmas and solutions with you, but also to teach you to ride the powerful wave of wine knowledge quickly, so you won't end up topless and embarrassed at the wine "shore!" This, we admit, is how we often found ourselves at the beginning of our wine journey!

This book will skim you along the most awesome waves of wine knowledge from a woman's perspective, and of course, make sure you look good when you're ready to go solo.

Dive in! See how fast and easy *Wine Chic Women* teaches you how to take hold of wine knowledge. Taste and experience the passion of wine, and share it with others. Who knows? You might just meet someone who'll be your next best friend!

Table of Contents

Acknowledgements

Finding ourselves in an industry dominated by ratings, somme-
liers and politics, we found ourselves confused, intimidated and
driven to write a book for ordinary women filled with information
for wine dilemmas, solutions and budgets. Writing a book is not a
simple task, and our book wouldn't be possible without the commu-
nity of hard-working people behind the scenes that helped make it
happen. We'd like to take this opportunity to thank them.

To our dear friend and editor, Beth Vasilakos, for her time, com-
mitment, patience and belief in our vision. We love you.

What's a book without a fabulous cover? We are most grateful to
Karne Dunshee for her incredibly chic cover design. We'd also like to
thank Rich Sommer, from It's All Digital, for his time and technical
expertise for graphically embedding and laying out the book.
Thanks also to Mary Ann Verderber for her incredible eye for photo
shots.

We are indebted to Robert Veitch for all of his guidance, wis-
dom, support and humor throughout the past couple of years.

We thank Dan Daul, Account Executive of Quality Wine and
Spirits, the original key, who helped put the concept of Novel Wines
into motion. We also appreciate the encouragement and support

from Brad Musolf, Regional Wine Manager for Trinchero Family Estates, for supporting a concept ahead of its time, and from Brian Bluhm, Store Manager and Company Wine Buyer of Top Ten Wine and Spirits, for embracing our initial concept. Thank you to Jeff Lavers, for his marketing direction, friendship and shared passion of wine.

Many thanks go out to Nick Fauchald, our first magazine editor, who gave us our initial opportunity to put our creative spin on wine.

These acknowledgements would not be complete without recognizing *Minnesota Monthly*, Kowalski's and The Chef's Gallery, for giving Sneakers and Heels a voice.

Thanks to Saint Croix Vineyards, Tiramisu and Top Ten Wine and Spirits for allowing us photo opportunities on their sites.

On a personal note, Jolie would like to thank her husband, Kurt, children, Robert and Alexa, and mom, Joyce, for their continued love, patience and support throughout writing this book. Jolie is also grateful to Carolyn, her sister-in-law, for her part in the original conception of Sneakers and Heels.

Lisa is most grateful to her husband, Chris, who supported her passion and children, Lauren and Madison, for allowing mom to spend all the extra time away from them. You are my angels.

Lastly, we raise our glasses to each other and clink to all those "No's." Cheers!

Introduction

Have you ever wanted to buy a wine book written *for* women, *by* women and tailored in a manner in which you can relate to quickly? We did, too! Keep in mind: we're two semi-normal, married women with young children and 18 years combined wine experience, who really love wine! Like most women, we are multi-tasking on a daily basis. We specifically wrote and designed the book to be read in time-pressed moments, although it can also be experienced while enjoying a quiet evening at home.

A wine image makeover will transform your wine knowledge from wine geek to wine chic using creative techniques and practical advice. You'll gain a deeper understanding of how to buy, cook with and order wine confidently. As you start to apply your new knowledge, you'll find yourself happily strutting through aisles of wine and restaurant wine lists. Never again will you solely rely on others to choose and enjoy good wine. Get ready! Your new wine image will turn heads and make mouths drop!

To help you maintain your new wine image, we've provided creative, yet simple, ways to remember this information. For instance, look for *Winescopes* in the first chapter. These are playful wine tidbits to help you identify the characteristics of wine varietals. There's even a wine-buying formula located in the book to assist you when shopping for wine. We will also introduce you to Novel Wines images. These wine reviews take the characteristics of wine and bring them to life.

Realizing our own wine budgets and dilemmas, the concept of Sneakers and Heels was first conceived on our website, http://www.novelwines.com, in order to enable women with or without budgets to learn more about wine. Sneakers and Heels are a natural spin-off of the personal wine experiences we've encountered. Sneakers is tight with the purse strings and always looking for bargains on wines. Heels is more discriminating about the impression and quality the wine leaves on the palate, and how the pricing compares to the competition. Think of Sneakers and Heels as your wine-savvy gal pals to whom you reach out for wine advice whenever you feel the need. Look for their wine tips scattered throughout this book.

We've found that one of the best ways to learn about wine and food is to jot down your wine encounters. At the end of each chapter, you will find different kinds of note-taking pages. Use them as worksheets. For example, Vintage Notes can be found at the end of Chapter 1. Keep track of good and bad vintages on this page so you can quickly refer to it before buying wine.

By recording your notes in this book, you'll know where they are and be able to refer to them quickly. And on that note, girlfriends...*get ready to lift your wine confidence to new elevations, renew your wine image and become wine chic women!*

Chapter 1-The Makeup of Wine

The Colorful Characteristics of Grape Varietals

Before we begin your new wine makeover, for just a moment, try envisioning some of the characteristics you might find in your friends. Some are thin, heavy, golden blonde, beautiful, deeply perfumed, dark or maybe somewhat exotic. Other friends might be sassy, seductive, short, loud, temperamental, rich, assertive, sophisticated or strong in character. Believe it or not, these are some of the same characteristics used to describe wine varietals—the different types of grapes used to make wine.

As you begin to sip different wine varietals, try having some fun and label them to a friend that you may know (male or female). The next time you come across that wine in a restaurant or wine shop, you'll think of your friend and remember the characteristics of that varietal.

There are many different wine varietals, but to keep it simple, only a basic few will be addressed. Descriptive personality characteristics will follow each grape varietal along with a suggested

Winescope pairing for the occasion. Winescopes are fun wine tidbits to playfully identify people or situations to help you remember the wine varietal characteristics. Which wine personality are you?

Chardonnay

These white wines tend to be dry, heavy in body and even somewhat fruity. They are rich and powerful, even somewhat aggressive—characteristics that make them stand apart from other white wines. In cool growing climates, chardonnay grapes tend to shout out apple and lemon; in hot growing regions, they smoothly exude peach, pineapple and even tropical fruits. Most chardonnay wines should be consumed within four years. *Winescope: Your most rich and powerful extroverted friends may become even more so if served this wine. Why not try it with some extremely shy friends to open them up a little?*

Sauvignon Blanc

These medium-bodied white wines tend to be crisp. They can be a little green and dry at times, but their brisk display of citrus fruit makes for wonderful dinner companions with most white meat. Sauvignon Blanc wines do not get better with age, so drink up. *Winescope: Most of the time, these wines give an honest fresh impression, which is quite nice when you're meeting that special someone for the very first time. Experience its innocence while sitting under a large oak tree on a grassy berm.*

Pinot Gris/Pinot Grigio

This pink grape is a sister of the Pinot family. The wines are typically straw-colored with a thin to medium body. The pear, apricot and citrus fruits strut their stuff with a crisp, tart attitude. These wines like to rock and roll with white fish and poultry. They should be consumed immediately. *Winescope: Imagine a thin, blonde rock star with big, pouty lips strutting across the stage. This tart will sing to all your rock star wannabe friends.*

Riesling

These beautiful white wines are sweet and heavily perfumed with floral, peach, apricot, apple and even lime zest. The big and full expensive Riesling wines tend to come from Germany and their beauty—ageless. Finer Rieslings have the distinct odor of gasoline. While it's not the most appealing of smells, after one sip you'll fool your brain into wanting more! The less expensive ones should be consumed right away. *Winescope: Think of your elder female relative coming for a visit in her pretty floral dress and matching hat, wafting of perfume and kissing everyone in sight. Share this love at family affairs.*

Gewurztraminer

Wines from this varietal are full-bodied, golden blonde and exotically fruity. Their distinctive perfume is seductive, throwing off swirls of kiwi, mango and grapefruit. They are extremely friendly with food. You'll often see these wines sitting side by side with a Thanksgiving turkey. *Winescope: Once you meet this exotic, gorgeous*

wine, its taste and perfume will be permanently etched into your senses.
Make a statement and serve this wine at any salad luncheon.

Semillon (Dessert Wines)

Dessert, anyone? Try these wines in place of dessert. Semillon grapes (sometimes blended with Sauvignon Blanc) make sweet, fat-bodied wines but become really intense when it to comes to showing their fruit. This intense fruitiness is because they are botrytized, meaning a fungus has been left to grow on them. The result is grapes that are high in sugar, fruit and acid. If grapes are allowed to freeze on the vine, *ice wine* is produced. Ice wines are sharp-witted but extremely sweet. *Winescope: Think of a sweet friend who's a little over-weight and really intense when it comes to stimulating conversation. Use this wine as an intermission.*

Pinot Noir

This grape is extremely moody when it comes to growing, mak-ing for some temperamental vintages. If the climate becomes too cool, the grapes will become thin and faint; if it's too warm, they get all jammed up in taste. When the climate is just so, these wines become soft-spoken and provocative, dropping hints of strawberry, cherry, violet, wood and spice. They are medium-to full-figured and sometimes a little on the fruity side. Their friendship is true with most fish dishes. Most Pinot Noir wines are ready to drink right away, though excellent vintages can be cellared for a short period of time. Vintage research is advised before buying any of these wines, since they are so fickle during their growing cycle. *Winescope: Do you*

have a shaky business or personal relationship that is extremely tempera-
mental? Simply serve an outstanding vintage; its smooth seduction will
be positively memorable, and the future will be yours to hold.

Merlot

These wines are naturally pretty and earthy. Merlots are full-bodied, and the more expensive ones drip with dark, rich fruit. Although they may seem like a family relation to the Cabernet Sauvignon grape family (and are commonly blended into Cabernet Sauvignon wines), Merlots are not as showy. These wines play out soft notes of plum and black currant. Finer Merlots can be stored for 4-8 years. *Winescope: This is like your naturally beautiful friend who wears nothing but Birkenstocks on her feet because "they're comfortable." It's a satisfying wine for just about everyone and everything, even ham-burgers.*

Syrah or Shiraz (Australian equivalent)

Get ready for some smoke and dark berry magic. Red wines from these grapes are deep and dark-colored, billowing out puffs of smoke, raspberry, spicy pepper and leather. In Australia, Shiraz is blended with the Cabernet Sauvignon grape. Most of the Australian Shiraz wines need to be consumed immediately. A more expensive Syrah from an outstanding vintage can be cellared longer. *Winescope: This dark-skinned, sultry jazz singer croons best in smoky nightclubs. Invite some of your more mysterious friends over and smoke out their true personalities with some Syrah, barbeque and jazz.*

Zinfandel or Primitivo (Italian equivalent)

These thick, muscular-bodied wines are full of sculpted raspberry and blackberry fruit. Some even exude chocolate. These grapes also are grown in large numbers to produce the pale wines known as "blush" or White Zinfandel. White Zinfandel wines have thin bodies and display a sweet side. Primitivo wines tend to pump up plummy, earthy and cherry scents. Zinfandels are fast-moving operators, willing to adapt to just about any robust party food. The high alcohol content (which gives them their spicy edge) makes for a wine that is fun, loud and flirtatious. Higher-priced Zinfandels can be extremely big, smooth and rich in texture. These finer wines have the ability to pull you away from whatever it is you were previously drinking and suck you into their seductive nature. Expensive Zinfandels can be stored from 4-8 years. *Winescope: Due to the seductive nature of these wines, it is ill-advised to serve them to the overly friendly and flirtatious people in your life. Instead, let your own hair down, light the fire and get ready to become a smooth operator with the love in your life.*

Cabernet Sauvignon

These grapes are thick-skinned, meaning the younger the wine, the more tannic—a noticeable astringency that is detectable by the dry, puckery feeling in your mouth. As the wine ages, the tannins will smooth out and become silky soft (think anti-wrinkle cream, girls). Cabernet Sauvignons cost more to produce because the vines produce low yields of grapes. Wines from these grapes are popular, jet-setting, strong in character, classical, beautiful and influential. Their fruit jewels are primarily cherry, red and black currant, accentuated by chocolate and licorice. Cabernets are made to age gracefully. Most New World Cabernet wines are produced to drink right away, with a small minority of exceptional producers making wines that can be cellared for years with proper storage. New World average cellar time is 4-8 years. Old World wines in an exceptional vintage can last 10 or more years. *Winescope: Drinking a beautiful classic Cabernet Sauvignon wine with a succulent beef tenderloin dinner can make anyone feel rich and powerful. Now share it all with your best friends and feel the love. What's more seductive than that?*

Sneakers and Heels Wine Tip: If the wine is expensive, it usually will age gracefully. Buy only the superior vintages to cellar. If the wine is a non-vintage (no year is shown on the bottle), the wine should be consumed immediately.

The Grapevine and Its Mood Swings

Like friendships, grapevines need to be nurtured and cared for in order to survive, mature and be fruitful. Some kinds of vines are easier to care for, whereas others might require daily attention and coddling. So that you can more fully understand how vines can become so different, we need to delve briefly into some technicalities of grapes and their grapevines.

In a vine's infancy, it's readily engaged in spreading out its root structure, too busy to worry about bearing any fruit. If neglected, the vine will go wild, bearing and dropping fruit here and there. The vine will continue to grow and reach out its long, woody fingers, constantly searching for something to wrap its twisted self around in order to climb higher. If the vine continues to mature in this untamed manner, it will eventually succumb to rot or pests.

Today, vines are not neglected. They are trained to grow, bud and mature under the strong guiding hands of the vintner (vine-grower), in accordance with the design plans of the vineyard. Vine growing is somewhat of an art. There are differing opinions on how high vine-growing posts should be, how many buds should be kept when pruning, how close to grow the vines together and even how far apart the rows should be in between the vines!

As the vine begins to mature, its roots reach out and dig deeper into the ground, searching for water and mineral sources. Deep root structure tends to protect it from drought. If planted in fast-draining soil, the roots will dig in faster. As the vine drinks in more of its environment (the terroir or microclimate), the grapes begin to produce wines that subtly reveal clues as to where they were grown. Different soils produce unique tastes that the more advanced wine drinker can identify.

After about five years, the vine starts producing a better quality of grapes. If a vine is lucky enough to reach its fully mature age of approximately thirty years old, it generally starts to produce less fruit thereafter and is designated an "old vine." These elder grapes command respect and produce outstanding premium wines. Their quality is reflected in the price of the wine, due to lower grape yields and high demand for superior grapes. Most of the time, though, these older vines are pulled out to make room for new vine plantings.

According to Napa Valley vineyard owners and winemakers, diseases and pests might prevent the vine from reaching its mature age of thirty. They say Phylloxera and Pierce's Disease are two common maladies that can be deadly to the vine. Phylloxera is a louse, first infecting the vine and eventually destroying the vine's root system. American vine roots are resistant to phylloxera, but European vines are not and need to be grafted onto American vines in order to protect them. Pierce's disease is a bacterium that is spread by an insect called a leaf hopper. Vines die within five years of infection. Unfortunately, there is no known cure for this disease.

Vintage Mood Swings

The grapevine's annual cycle is totally dependent on the weather. If any part of the annual expected season experiences freakish weather conditions, it can disturb or interrupt the vine's annual cycle. This, in turn, can make or break a vintage (the year of the actual grape harvest and the wine made from those grapes).

One of the most important seasons for the vine is its dormant period. Wouldn't it be nice if you could have a dormant period of uninterrupted sleep during your cycle? The grapevine must have this dormancy in order to thrive, thereby commanding where they can be grown in the world, since this deep sleep period is brought on by cold weather. While the vines sleep, vintners give them a winter pruning. This pruning tells the awakening vine how many grapes to produce and, consequently, has a tremendous effect on the quality of grapes. (Industry experts are convinced low-yielding grapevines produce high-quality grapes.) After their winter sleep, during a normal season, the buds begin to swell in March and break open in April. A freakish frost at this point in the cycle may affect the grapevine's quantity and/or quality, or it may kill the crop entirely.

In June, small flowers appear. The amount and date of flowering is a great indicator for the size and timing of the harvest (early blooms equal early harvest). The grapevine can be somewhat sensitive at this point, wanting lots of warmth and sunshine now. If, however, there is a lot of rain, the grapevine becomes depressed. If the vine is beaten severely at this point due to hail or high winds, not only will the weather wreck that year's vintage, but future vintages could also be affected.

Small grapes start to appear around July and continue to thrive throughout the summer. The biggest challenge for the vintner is when to harvest. September is typically the month, but again depending on the weather, harvest can go as late as October. Two variables determine when to harvest: the weather forecast and the build-up of sugar levels in the grapes. As the grapes ripen, the acidity falls and the fermentable sugars rise. In order to achieve perfect sugar levels, the vintners and their grapevines want dry weather from July all the way through the harvest.

> Sneakers and Heels Wine Tip: Did you know one ton of grapes makes approximately 60 cases of 750ml wine?

Old World and New World Wines

As you become more familiar with wine growing regions, you inevitably will come across the following terms: Old World wines and New World wines. Old World wines are wines that come from wine growing regions in countries that have been making wines for years, such as those in Europe. New World wines come from countries such as the U.S.A., Australia, New Zealand, South Africa and South America. The main difference is New World wines label their wines by varietal (Chardonnay, Merlot, Zinfandel), while Old World wines label by geographical wine region (Bordeaux, Chianti, Rhone). For example: You are not buying a Bordeaux varietal; you are buying the Cabernet Sauvignon varietal from the wine growing appellation of Bordeaux. It's much easier to figure out what you're drinking when the wine is labeled by varietal as are New World wines. Otherwise, when drinking a bottle from the Old World, you must know in advance what grape varietal is grown and produced in that specific wine-growing appellation. This information is a book in itself! A simple piece of advice: When starting out on your new wine journey, begin with New World wines and when you're comfortable with most of the varietals, start learning about Old World wines. A few wine regions have been selected in this book and divided into hot and cool regions. This helps explain how the weather affects the grapes and their vintages and can be used as a quick reference when buying wine.

Sneakers and Heels Wine Tip: It is important to know how the weather affected the grapevine's cycle in different wine regions in the world, in order to protect yourself from buying a wine from a bad vintage. Read wine magazines and surf the Internet for vintage information.

Cool Regions

Cool growing wine regions (in a normal growing year) allow the grapes to ripen slowly. Slow ripening permits the flavor and sugar contents to be high, making for near perfect grapes. Of course, this means wines from these cooler-growing regions are typically higher quality and more expensive!

A sampling of cool wine regions in California include Alexander Valley, Anderson Valley, Carneros, Chalk Hill, Mendocino, Monterey, Napa, Russian River Valley, Paso Robles and Sonoma. Cool regions in France include Bordeaux, Cote D'Or, Champagne and Rhone.

Hot Regions

In hot wine regions, grapes ripen faster in terms of sugar content but *not* in flavor. Envision it like buying apples in a grocery store. You pick what you think looks good in color and feel, but when you take a bite from one of those beautiful apples, sugar content is missing. The same goes for grapes in hot regions. These wines tend to be on the mediocre side, but they are also less costly. Unfortunately, the vintners in hot regions can't let these grapes ripen too far, as it makes for a wine that tastes like raisins or port.

A sampling of California's hot regions include: Amador, El Dorado, Fresno, San Joaquin, San Bernardino, San Diego and Sacramento. Southern Spain and North Africa are also hot wine growing areas.

Here's where vintage mood swings can come into play. A cool region might experience an unusually hot growing season, which in turn adversely affects the grapes. Those grapes will ripen just as if they were in a hot region, making wines from cool growing regions mediocre to poor that year. Unfortunately, you'll still be paying a hefty price for that mediocre wine, since most wineries don't adjust their prices for "off" years. Wouldn't you rather spend the same amount of money on a great wine from an outstanding year, rather than on a mediocre wine in a bad year?

How do you become wine region/vintage savvy? A good start is by reading wine magazines, newspapers and surfing the Internet. Remember to make it easy on yourself and start with New World wines first. Next, figure out how the weather affected the grapes that harvest season. Record your information on your Vintage Notes page, in a wine diary or on a computer. Highlight the good years in particular regions. Before you walk into any shop to buy wine, refer back to your notes. You'll be wine vintage/region savvy in no time flat!

> **Sneakers and Heels Wine Tip:** To avoid throwing yourself into your own mood swing, never assume a vintage you bought and loved last year will taste the same in another year. Another simple rule is never to buy a red wine over $40, unless you've tasted it, a wine friend has recommended it or you know from research that a particular vintage is a good one.

Worksheet
Vintage Notes

Keep track of good and bad vintages here.

Chapter 2-Mastering the Art of Wine and Food Application

Wine Contouring

Imagine you're facing an artist's easel with a clean canvas and someone places a brush in your hand. You exclaim, "I am not an artist!" Most people feel this way when trying to pair wine with food. Ah, but wait! There *is* a tasteful remedy. It's called wine contouring.

Wine contouring is the outlining of fruit characteristics in a particular wine. How do you do that? It's simple. You just create your own personal wine contouring kit. Here's how it's done:

- Start with a box of salt-free crackers to cleanse your palate: Don't expose your palate to any strong flavors such as toothpaste, mints or gum. Other palate killers are hot, spicy foods such as salsa or tobacco. Your taste buds will become shocked and unable to identify any fruit characteristics at all.

- Gather some fruits. In order to outline or pinpoint the dominant fruit in the wine, you need to have fruits on hand that display themselves in that particular varietal of wine. (Fresh fruit is ideal, but canned will do.) The fruit leader will dance on your palate once you find it. The fruit leader is the most dominant fruit, not necessarily the first fruit you taste. Remember, white wines typically display lighter-colored fruits such as green apple, pear, honey, grapefruit, peach and apricot. Red wines exhibit dark fruit like black and red cherry, currants, blackberry and raspberry. Think of the wine and fruits as your paint; you'll be blending those onto your palate (which *is* your palette in this case).

- Use two identical bottles of wine. One is for experimentation before planning your dinner and one is for serving with the actual dinner.

- Have specific food on hand that you want to sample with the wine. Beginners should apply the basic white wine, white meat or red wine, red meat principle. (Refer to the Wine and Food Pairings Table.) As you become more comfortable, you can start to mix white meat with red wine.

- Try some tasty food accents. Have like-color fruit marinades, cheeses, sauces and spices in the house to try with the wine. Fun ones to have on hand are fruit-based salsas, marinades and jams.

- Get some blank recipe cards. Record your favorite wine and food concoctions, making sure to write down exact proportions.

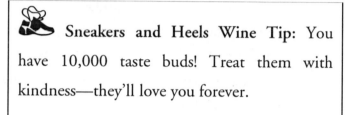

Sneakers and Heels Wine Tip: You have 10,000 taste buds! Treat them with kindness—they'll love you forever.

When applying Wine Contouring, think of it as a creative art form. In this case, art is a form of expression derived from the laughter and shadows of your heart. Some wine and food creations will be reflections of your moods; others will be based on time and practicality. If you feel you've stumbled onto a wine and food masterpiece, savor every bit of it, as no wine and food experience can ever be precisely replicated.

Here are Wine Contouring instructions so you can experiment with your own creations:

1. Choose one fruit at a time. Then sip the wine with each fruit, until you've outlined its fruit leader(s). As you sip the wine, ask yourself the following questions: What do I taste

in the forward, or first, part of the sip? Is there a particular fruit jumping out right away? Next, see what the wine tastes like in the middle of the sip. Is it becoming drier, sweeter, dying off? Is the fruit changing to a different flavor? Lastly, how is the finish? What do you taste now? Did the finish fade right away or is it still seductively hanging around on your palate trying to get you to taste some more? In a quality wine, you want the forward, middle and finish to all be present on your palate. If the forward part, for example, is all fruit up front but nothing on the finish (the finish died immediately), it's a sign that the vines from which these grapes were harvested produced large yields. Therefore, the quality of these grapes has been significantly diminished.

2.   Using sauces and marinades similar to the fruit characteristics of the wine, try each separately with the wine. Cleanse your palate in between each wine with salt-free crackers and water.

3.   Combine one of your tasty accents with the specific food. Take a sip of the wine. Some combinations will overpower the wine's flavor, and some will dramatically enhance it.

4.   Don't forget to sample a couple of different cheeses with the wine, too!

5. Record your wine and food pairings at the end of this chapter or on a blank recipe card.

6. HAVE FUN!

Sneakers and Heels Wine Tip: When pairing wine with food, dress them alike. Heavier foods need heavier-bodied wines; lighter foods need lighter-bodied wines. Too heavy of a food will overpower a lighter-bodied wine and vice versa.

Wine and Food Pairings Table

Below is a basic novice wine and food table to help guide you through it all. As you begin to pair wine and food, stick with the simple rule of white meat, white wine and red meat, red wine. Once you feel comfortable, start to apply spices, marinades and sauces to the food. Try mixing a red wine with different white meats by adding a red fruit-based sauce, marinade or salsa. A simple trick is to always make sure you match the color of your sauce to your wine. For example: You've grilled some chicken and want to top it with a hot red raspberry preserve sauce. Your red raspberry sauce will need a red wine that exhibits primarily raspberry fruit characteristics.

FOOD	WINE VARIETALS
Chicken, turkey, fish, shellfish, white-sauced pasta, Chinese food, pesto pasta	White wines: Sauvignon Blanc, Pinot Grigio, Riesling, Gewurztraminer
Salmon, tuna, turkey, pork, ham, roast, BBQ	Red wines: Pinot Noir, Shiraz/Syrah, Zinfandel
Steak, pizza, bruschetta, red-sauced pasta, chocolate	Red wines: Merlot, Zinfandel, Cabernet Sauvignon

Hot and Cold Temperature Flashes

To make a wine truly inviting, it is essential to serve it at the proper temperature. Most of the time, white wines are served too cold and red wines are served too warm. If a white wine has been in a food refrigerator longer than 15 minutes, it's too cold. If you're in a restaurant and the glass of white wine you've been served fogs over, it's a good indicator your wine is too cold. White wine should not be served this cold, as it causes the wine's fruits to cover up; its aroma and bouquet will be unable to release their pleasures to your senses.

If you're served a wine that's too cold, here's what you do: Wrap your hands around the bowl of the glass and hold them there for a few minutes. Like magic, the wine's characteristics will begin to emerge from the frosty depths and come alive on your palate. Once this occurs, introduce the wine to your food.

An even more difficult situation is red wine being served too warm. This also is a sign that the wine may have been improperly stored. Not knowing the length of time that wine has not been stored properly makes it difficult to determine if the wine has been damaged. The body and character of the wine might be changed from what it should be or even tainted. Whenever you enter a restaurant, become a wine detective; look around and see where the wine is located and how it's being stored. If the bottles are stored in a beverage refrigerator, you should have no problem with the quality or temperature of your wine. Beware of wines stored on a rack in the warmth of the dining room or, even worse, on a rack near the kitchen or dishwasher. The heat, light and vibrations of the environment can rapidly age a wine and eventually destroy it.

At the restaurant, as soon as the wine is brought to your table, touch the bottle. If it is not cool to the touch, it's too warm. Ask the server not to open it and to bring an ice bucket filled with half ice and half water. Place the bottle in the bucket for about 15 minutes. Then signal the server to come and open the bottle for a taste. Look at the cork.

Make sure the wine hasn't seeped up past the top of it. (If a wine is stored in continued high heat, it will not only age faster, but its cork will tend to swell and shrink, causing the airtight seal to be broken.) You'll know if the wine is off by its bitter taste.

The best place to store wine in the home (short of the perfect wine cellar with optimum temperature and humidity) is in your basement. An unfinished area in the basement with concrete walls is even better. Just make sure it's not next to the furnace, which will cause heat and vibrations. If you don't have a basement, it's highly recommended to store wine in the coolest place in your house, away from any direct light. You could also invest in a small beverage refrigerator, especially if you have any desire to start a wine collection. These wine fridges don't become as cold as food refrigerators, and you can set the temperature to between 50-60 degrees Fahrenheit—optimum storage temperature for wine.

If you have any white wine leftover from the evening, stick the cork back in and put it on the shelf of your refrigerator door. Make sure to pull it out approximately 30 minutes before serving. The wine should last about two days. Red wine can be stored on the counter but should be consumed the very next evening; anything after that is on borrowed time unless you use a wine preserver system. These systems will be explained in Chapter 6.

Sneakers and Heels Wine Tip: Having a hot flash? Here's what to do: pour yourself a cool dessert wine, sip on it as you make your way into the lukewarm shower, then cover yourself with peppermint body soap! Rinse with cold water. There are no guarantees here, girls!

Worksheet
Favorite Wine and Food Contouring Applications

Record your wine and food concoctions while they're still fresh in your mind.

Chapter 3-Solving Seven Common Wine Dilemmas

We are often in charge of buying wine when cooking, entertaining, or attending a party. How many times have you found yourself wondering what wine to serve or take to gatherings, parties and dinners? Here are seven common wine dilemmas all paired with solutions.

Wine Dilemma #1: A Summer Party

The invitation reads:

Who: Jenny and Joe Smith

What: Dinner Party

Where: Smith's House

Why: Celebrate Summer's Arrival

PS: Bring a bottle of wine to share

What wine do you bring to share?

Solution: First, call the host to find out what main entrée will be served. If you don't call ahead, it's like going to a party without your makeup on. The purpose of the call is to pinpoint what wine will match best with the food being served. Remember to find out if the entrée will be grilled, baked or spicy and whether it will be topped with any marinade or sauce. You are being considerate by asking these questions, and the host will only see you as wine-savvy.

Wine Dilemma #2: The Special Birthday

The invitation reads:

What: Celebrate John's 40th

Where: John and Mary's house at 7:00 p.m.

(Please, no gifts.)

John and Mary are your closest friends. You wouldn't dream of *not* bringing a gift. He loves wine.

Solution: Red wine is always best since it ages longer. Since he loves wine and it's a special birthday, spend around $30-80 for a bottle of red, depending on your budget (you could split the cost with someone). Do a little of your own research before buying the wine and make sure it was a good to outstanding vintage before spending this kind of money. Try hitting a wine shop that is known for its wine expertise. Shop here during the weekday between 1:30 p.m. and 3:30 p.m. Then, ask for the wine manager. This is the time of day when the wine manager is usually available and able to spend some personal time with you. Avoid wine shop rush hour, which is between 5:00 p.m. and 7:00 p.m. Finding someone with wine knowledge at this hour is virtually impossible. Zinfandel or Cabernet Sauvignon is a safe bet. For an extra nice touch, throw in a couple of porterhouse steaks!

Sneakers and Heels Wine Tip: Heels special occasion cellar wines include star-studded reds such as: Chalk Hill Cabernet Sauvignon, Darioush Cabernet Sauvignon, Domaine Serene Pinot Noir, Far Niente Cabernet Sauvignon, Guilliams Cabernet Sauvignon, Jarvis Cabernet Sauvignon, Jordan Cabernet Sauvignon, Pride Merlot, Provenance Cabernet Sauvignon, Richard Partridge Cabernet Sauvignon, Simi Cabernet Sauvignon, and Turley Zinfandel—all heavy hitters to impress the best! Buy only the best vintages.

Wine Dilemma #3: On a Budget

You're newly married and strapped for cash. New friends are coming for lasagna, and they love wine. What wine do you serve, and how do you keep from looking "wine ignorant?"

Solution: Dish out the pasta on your new fine china, but forget about serving wine in the fancy etched crystal wine glasses. "Excuse me?" you ask. Just why did you get those expensive crystal wine glasses then? Good question! The etching and small bowls of crystal wine glasses only make it harder to swirl the wine (swirling releases the aroma and fragrant bouquet of the wine), to clearly see the wine's color. If you want to look wine-savvy, buy four uncolored, big-bowled wine glasses, and serve your wine in them. They're usually around $3-4 a piece. Watch for sales to buy more glasses in the future. What do you serve in your fancy etched crystal wine glasses? Dessert! Try cutting up cubes of Brie and layer the cubes with raspberries and blueberries parfait-style in the crystal wine glasses. Top with a couple of fresh raspberries, blueberries and a mint leaf. An $8-10 bottle of Shiraz or Zinfandel will hold up to any lasagna, and yet be perfect with your elegant dessert!

Wine Dilemma #4: The Boss

The boss is coming to dinner for the first time.

Solution: Don't panic! First, figure out your main entrée. How are you going to prepare it? Why not try one of your new fruit marinade concoctions over some chicken or fish? Determine your side dishes last. Make sure to keep the spices to a minimum. Next, determine what appetizers you're going to serve. It's helpful to choose appetizers that will need white and red wines. This way you have either a red or white wine to save the day. Try serving meatballs, hard cheese and cracker assortments, accompanying them with white and red fruits such as pear, pineapple, red grapes, blackberries, raspberries and strawberries. To prevent the boss from experiencing a wine fashion "don't," have the table preset with additional wine glasses for dinner and pour some of the new dinner wine into the glasses. Make sure you have at least two bottles of your dinner wine on hand in order to give maximum coverage throughout the entire meal.

Wine Dilemma #5: Hosting a Party

You're hosting a "home" party, book club or holiday gathering.

How much wine do you need, what kind do you buy, and what do

you serve with it?

Solution: There are six full glasses of wine that can be poured per bottle or one bottle per person, depending on your crowd! Keep in mind the average person drinks about two glasses of wine at a gathering. Make sure everyone goes home with a full stomach of food. Next, determine what foods you can serve that will be wine-friendly. For instance, buy a wheel of Brie and top with mixed berry jam and place fresh dark fruits on the top of it. Place a food and wine pairing suggestion card in front of each bottle of wine such as: Try this wine with the Brie wheel. Make it easy on yourself and serve appetizers only. Assume half of your guests will drink red and half will drink white wine. Best dollar value wines include whites such as Pinot Grigio and Sauvignon Blanc, and reds such as Zinfandel and Shiraz. Don't use plastic wine glasses at your party. If you don't have enough wine glasses, rent or borrow some. Nothing cheapens your hostess image more than having boxed wine and plastic wine glasses. There are plenty of reasonably-priced quality wines to choose from that are bottled. Remember, watch your guests and designate a driver if someone has had too much fun experimenting with wines at your party.

Sneakers and Heels Wine Tip: Psst...Sneakers' favorite party wines are Beringer Founder's Estate Cabernet Sauvignon, Marietta Old Vine Zinfandel, Montevina Pinot Grigio and Trinchero Sauvignon Blanc.

Wine Dilemma #6: Girlfriends and PMS

Your girlfriend calls and tells you her child is flunking math, her husband is going on a two-week international trip tomorrow and the dog visit to the veterinarian just cost $250. She's on fire and smoldering in PMS.

What do you do?

Solution: You can either hang up and avoid her for the next two weeks, or arm yourself with Zinfandel and raspberry chocolate bars. High tail it on down to her house immediately. Zinfandel has enough attitude to put out any PMS fires.

Wine Dilemma #7: The Housewarming

You've just been invited to a housewarming for your new neighbors. You don't know them at all.

Solution: Are you worried they might not drink wine? Not to fret! If they don't partake in wine, they'll inevitably know someone who does enjoy it. Stay in the $10-12 range. Merlot or Shiraz keeps you on neutral footing, and it's versatile and food friendly. Who knows, maybe they'll pay you the highest compliment and open up your bottle at their housewarming.

Sneakers and Heels Wine Tip: When faced with potential wine dilemmas, eliminate them by having the answers to the "wine trinity" questions: what food or main entrée is being served, what kind of wine does it need (red or white) and what fruit characteristics will the wine display? Soon, your dilemmas will become logical and educated wine successes.

Worksheet
Your Wine and Food Dilemmas

Write down other wine and food dilemmas. Send them to us!

Chapter 4-Removing Wine Buying Barriers

Walking into a wine shop can be intimidating, not to mention humiliating, especially if you think your wine image is not up to snuff. Before you step foot into any wine shop, it's helpful to understand the wine buying ABCs, wine shop organization and how to shop wines sales.

Wine Buying ABCs

Wine buying is simple if you keep A, B and C in mind.

- *Always* know why you're buying wine. Are you buying wine for a special occasion, dinner or party?

- *Before* you go shopping for wine, know whether you'll need a red or white wine. If you're buying for a special occasion, red is best since these wines tend to age longer and are natural foundation pairings for food. If you're headed to a dinner party, call ahead and ask the host what main entrée is being served. Remember to ask how it will be prepared. Will it be grilled, baked or spicy? If it is a spicy dish, you'll need a little sweeter wine to cool the heat. If you're hosting a dinner party or gathering, plan your menu first, then buy the wine.

• *Cost* needs to be factored into your decision. Determine what you want to spend on the wine. Pick a price point and stay within $5 of it. The special occasion wines cost a little more; try staying around $30-60. Again, red wine is your best option. If you're going to a dinner party, spend between $10-20. There are many high-quality wines in this category, therefore increasing your odds of getting a good bottle and not offending your host with a cheap bottle of wine (especially if they know wine). Keep the price tag on your wines when storing them so you can reference how much it cost before consuming it. Of course, never forget to remove the price tag before giving or serving it.

Organization of a Wine Shop

Most wine shops have wines organized according to the wine shop owner's preference and what niche the shop is trying to fill. For example, maybe the shop has a California flare. Frequent a shop that is accommodating and become familiar with its layout, just like you do the grocery store. Most stores have wines grouped into domestic and foreign areas. Until you are comfortable in a wine shop, stick to the domestic section. The labels are all in English and listed by varietal (Chardonnay, Merlot, etc.). Typically, expensive wines are on top, with cheaper wines on the bottom. You may notice a special wine room in some wine shops. This area is where the really expensive and hard-to-find wines can be found. Go in and have a look around. Become familiar with some of the labels and prices.

Throughout the shop, you may notice stacked cases of certain wines on the floor. This is similar to a restaurant's daily special; the wine shop bought a lot of it and now wants you to buy it. Some of these wines are absolute gems. Some are duds. This is when it becomes important to have a wine relationship with a manager you can trust. Once you find a wine manager or advisor you like, stick with him or her like you would your hairstylist! Learn what hours they work and call ahead to make sure they're working on the day you need them to help you. Most wine managers are accessible weekdays between 1:00 p.m. and 3:00 p.m.

Shopping a Wine Sale

Wine shops have sales to draw you into their store, move old inventory and introduce new wine vintages. Refer to your notes on different wine regions, if the wine shop is moving out older vintages. Find out what regions had outstanding, good and poor vintages.

Think about your wine needs for the next six months. (The really good wine sales happen every six months.) Are you hosting any large parties? Are there any special occasions coming up? How many guiltless wines do you need on hand? (Guiltless wines are $10 and under.)

Here's a great wine-buying formula to use when shopping a wine sale. First, how many guiltless wines do you consume per week? Let's assume two bottles. Next, multiply that by four. This gives you the number of guiltless wines you drink a month. Now multiply that by six. This is the number of wines you'll need to have on hand for the next six months.

---

2 bottles x 4 weeks = 8 bottles   8 bottles x 6 months = 48 bottles

---

Remembering that there are 12 bottles in a case of wine, you'll need to buy four cases of wine at the sale. When buying the four cases, mix the varietals according to the foods you eat most. If you eat mostly red meat dishes, you'll need to have a heavier emphasis on red wines and vice versa.

For special occasion wines, try buying three to six bottles (depending on your budget) and stay around $30 a piece (sale price). Some of your better buys at sales can be found on the higher end wines. Keep in mind, you might want to go to the sale twice: once to buy your special occasion wine and once for your guiltless wines. Special occasion wines typically sell out during the first few days of a sale.

Be wary of large wine displays at sales. Large quantity doesn't necessarily mean good quality. Watch vintages carefully at sales, and stick with buying wines of the vintages you've researched. If there is no vintage listed on the label, it's a blend of different vintages. For example, in the United States, a wine label gets to list its vintage only if 95 percent of a wine's grapes come from grapes harvested that year. Be aware that wine shop clerks might try to push a less than successful vintage on you. If in doubt about a particular vintage, ask them to open a bottle (especially if you're buying more than a case) to make sure you like it. This is standard industry etiquette when buying large quantities of wine. If the clerk balks or is unaccommodating, this is not the shop or sale for you! Take your business elsewhere.

Use the wine sales to your advantage. Try some new wines for free! Most shops have free wine tasting samples throughout the shop. Just make sure you write down which ones you like and why for future reference. There are usually wine representatives on hand during large sales. You might be lucky enough to even meet a winemaker. Make sure you introduce yourself to any wine representative. Tell them you are eager to learn more about wine and have them tell you a little about their wines. If one of the winemakers is on hand, take advantage of this rare opportunity. Ask them how the wine was made and what any future release vintages taste like in the barrel. This is a clue as to how good these wines will be before they are even bottled. You can even have the winemaker sign a bottle of the wine you're buying. Wine representatives are extremely friendly and always willing to talk wine. It's their passion, too! Make sure to get on the wine shop's mailing list. This way you'll know about any future wine tasting, private sales, wine clubs and extra discounts.

> **Sneakers and Heels Wine Tip:** Never buy a wine simply because it has a pretty label, unless you're specifically out to make oil candles out of the wine bottles. Many great wines are packaged with the most simple of labels.

At the Warehouse

Like groceries, wines now can be purchased warehouse-style. Warehouse wines are found in stores like Sam's Club, Costco and Cost Plus, to name a few. Wines available in these warehouses are usually mainstream name-brand wines and widely produced. Usually, these kinds of wines can be bought daily at below the cost of small wine shop sale prices. Wine warehouses are all about moving large quantities of wine. There are no frills, wine sales or tastings. Don't count on any sales clerk for a wine recommendation. The only reason you should be buying wine from a warehouse is because you've previously tasted the wine, (knowing its quality, vintage and price), you're confident in the wines you're purchasing or you're hosting a large gathering.

Guiltless wines are everywhere. If you see a bottle that's from a name-brand winery for $5 and it was a great vintage, buy one. Take it home and see if you like it. You might just find a new guiltless wine.

If you're spending more than $15 on a bottle of wine in a warehouse, remember these wines have not necessarily been stored in ideal temperature or humidity-controlled environments. Bottles are typically stored upright, too, which could cause a corkage problem, tainting the wine. However, some high-end rare wines can be found at substantial savings. If the wine is over $15, it's best to buy one bottle first to try at home. If it's good, go back and buy more, but don't keep it in long-term storage since its storage history is unknown. Consume it within the next few months.

Make sure to check monthly to see if any new inventory has arrived, and be sure to visit around the holidays. The warehouses tend to carry exclusive wine gift pack sets not found in other wine shops. These wine gift packs might be just the thing for clients or friends!

Sneakers and Heels Wine Tip: Sneakers says dress down and wear a baseball hat to shop wine at warehouses. This clearly puts you in the right frame of mind to find bargains. Look for guiltless wines only. Check the stacked cases of wines carefully for vintages. Don't you dare buy any boxed wine! Heels says wear designer jeans, and look for red wines in good vintages, between $15-25 and white wines between $15-20. Remember, if any wine is over $30, buy only one bottle to take home and sample.

Worksheet
Preferred Wine Shops, Managers and Sales

Chronologically order all wine sales and note your favorite wine personnel.

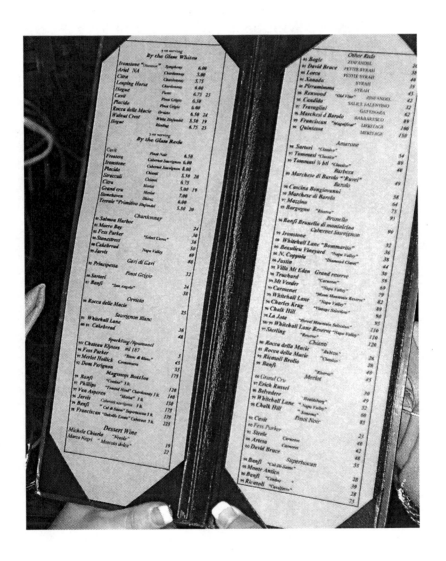

Chapter 5-Trying on Wines in a Restaurant

Trying on wine with the wrong food can be similar to trying on swimsuits—the fluorescent lights and mirrors have a "fun house" effect on your body. For example: The smoked salmon appetizer you've ordered arrives at your table along with your glass of Cabernet Sauvignon. It *looks* fabulous! You take a bite of the appetizer and try on a sip of the wine. What's your palate's image of this pairing? You've just eaten a rotten piece of fish from a trashcan. This is due to a chemical reaction clashing with the high tannins found in certain red wines; the effect is a metallic-like taste. Your palate is devastated.

Fortunately, there are not too many foods that have this severe of a reaction, but there are plenty of moderate to mild mismatched reactions that can have devastating effects on your palate. This is why it's so important *not* to order wine before you've ordered food in a restaurant. Think of it like this: You don't buy a string bikini, hoping your body's going to fit in it, right?

Odds are you've already experienced some wine fashion "don'ts" as stated above. These wine mistakes might have been experienced on a night when you sent your food back because it didn't taste quite right. Or you feel the food at your favorite restaurant hasn't been quite up to snuff, and you haven't been back since (which could be true). Wine and food pairing can make or destroy a meal. Once you experience and are aware of the excellent wine and food matches, it'll become second nature to you, kind of like pairing jelly with peanut butter. Following are common wine encounters you may face when dining in a restaurant.

Three Wine Encounters in a Restaurant

You've just been seated at your table. The wine list and menus are placed in front of you. Nine times out of ten, the server comes by within seconds to see if you'd like to order a drink. The server knows you've not had time to look at the menu yet.

This is the first encounter. The servers are asking if you'd like a drink before you've had chance to look at the menu. Go ahead; order a social glass of wine to enjoy! Don't necessarily consider this your wine for dinner. Before requesting a second glass of wine, wait until you know what you're ordering as your entrée. This prevents you from being stuck with a full glass of wine that is not going to fit with your food.

Your second encounter is when you are presented the wine list. You start to feel the restaurant "wine list panic." Wine list panic is like walking on the deck of a pool or beach for the first time in your new swimsuit; all eyes feel like they're on you. The server is extremely busy and is practically standing on top of you. *Don't* give in to this pressure or you'll end up ordering your usual wine, which may not go with the food and decreases your odds of having an excellent wine and food pairing. Besides, you don't even know what your main entrée is yet. To avoid this panic, just tell the server you're going to need a few minutes.

Maybe you've decided to put the server on the spot and ask for a wine recommendation. This is your third encounter. Don't ask the server for a recommendation until you know what you're ordering. Once you know, then ask your server for a recommendation and tell them approximately what you want to spend. Here is an insider tip: Most restaurant food servers are told to ask you what your favorite wine is first, then make a recommendation based on your answer. This method of recommendation isn't always a good thing, since your favorite wine might not be a wine that pairs well with your food. What to do? Go ahead and tell them what your favorite wine is, then tell them you're more interested in knowing what wine will go best with the entrée. Hopefully, this recommendation will now be based on the food, your taste and the price. If you still aren't quite sure about the server's recommendation, have them ask the chef for a recommendation.

> **Sneakers and Heels Wine Tip:** You'll get the best wine recommendations from restaurant wine sommeliers, who are educated in wine and food pairings. Unfortunately, wine sommeliers are usually only found in upscale restaurants. All the more reason for increasing your own wine/food pairing knowledge!

Restaurant Wine List Browsing: Wine Suit Logic

When in a barrel-sized dressing room piled high with 10 or maybe even 15 swimsuit choices, you set an automatic buying system into motion. This consists of two piles: the "not a chance" and the "maybe" piles. Why should buying wine in a restaurant (which costs just about as much as a swimsuit) be any different? Now that you have the wine list in hand, first decide what you're going to eat. Let's say you're going to have blackened chicken. For now, remember the simple rule of white meat, white wine. Most restaurants have already sorted the wines into piles of white and reds. Upscale restaurants have a more structured wine list, but that's when the sommelier comes in handy.

Find the white wines. Next, choose a price point. Let's say you want to stay around $30. Eliminate all wines that don't fall within five dollars of this amount. Chances are, you'll be left with about four wines.

Invite your server to come back; see if they have any knowledge about which of those wines would work best with the blackened chicken. If not, have them ask the chef or refer back to Chapter 1 and the grape varietal personalities. This just may be one of those times where you must learn by tasting the experience. There is no right or wrong answer.

Use Wine Suit Logic for wines by the glass. This may be necessary if three of you are having white wine, but the fourth needs a glass of red wine. For example, you're out with another couple. Here's what's ordered: grilled halibut, white-sauced pasta, stuffed feta chicken and beef tenderloin. When ordering a bottle of wine, majority rules. That doesn't mean you have to succumb and drink a white wine with your beef tenderloin! Instead, order a glass of red wine. Inquire about what's available by the glass in red wines. Decide what you want to spend on a glass of wine. Then eliminate the rest. You'll probably be left with two reasonable choices. It is perfectly acceptable to ask for a small taste of each wine. Keep in mind the wine's temperature. If the small taste of wine is too warm, the big glass will be even warmer! Kindly ask the server to stick the glass in the refrigerator for about five minutes, then bring it back to you. As you continue to use Wine Suit Logic for restaurant wine lists, you'll learn how easy it is to try on different kinds of wines comfortably and learn what works and what doesn't, not to mention dramatically increasing your odds of experiencing more wine fashion "do's."

Sneakers and Heels Wine Tip: Don't forget to record what you ate and with what wine in the Tasty Wine Encounters recording area of this book. Make sure you jot down everything from the front of the wine label, especially the type of wine varietal, year (vintage), country where produced and price. Use a napkin to write on if needed, and stick it in your purse so you can record the wine later.

Worksheet
The Restaurant Best Of: Wine Selection, Wine-By-the-Glass,
Wine Price and Advice

Chapter 6-Flaunting Your Wines-Accessory Must Haves

Your wine makeover is almost complete! Wine styling accessories are an essential investment to your wine-savvy image. Want to know the beauty of having wine as a hobby? You can spend as little or as much on it as you want! Here are eight wine accessories that are key in helping you live your new wine image.

Foil Cutters

Have you ever stopped and looked at the foil that covers the wine's bottleneck (technically called a capsule) and thought, "How do I get all this off and find the cork?" Maybe you've even grabbed a bottle of wine in the wine shop by the neck and had the foil move around on the bottle. Does this mean the wine is bad or the cork is not sealed properly? Here are your answers. If the foil moves around on the neck of the bottle, there is no need for alarm. The foil has nothing to do with whether or not the wine is sealed properly. Some wineries choose to put foil around their wines; others choose to seal the cork with a dip in hot wax. It's more of an aesthetic marketing choice for wineries, though the foil capsule does add some extra protection to the cork. You can get to the cork via three ways. You can clumsily tear off all of the foil, (which is an amateurish wine faux pas in itself), try cutting the foil off (or your finger) with a knife or lastly, invest in a foil cutter. To use the foil cutter, place it on top of the bottleneck, making a quarter of a turn and presto! Your foil has been precisely cut off into a perfect circle; the cork is now exposed. Sneakers has some good news. These foil cutters will only set you back about $3 and save you a possible trip to the emergency room!

Electronic Wine Chillers and Warmers

Bathe your wine bottle in its correct serving temperature simply by investing in an electronic wine chiller. All you have to do is plug it in, preset the temperature and insert your bottle! When the bottle reaches the desired temperature, a light will illuminate. Heels loves this accessory for serving wine on a hot summer night.

Vacuum Pump Wine Preserver Systems

Let's say you've opened up a bottle of wine but only poured one glass from it. Will your wine still be good the next day? You'll increase the odds of preserving it if you invest in some sort of a wine preserver system. One Sneakers budget item is a vacuum pump preserver. Oxidation causes wines to spoil. The vacuum pump removes virtually all of the air from the bottle, preserving some wines for up to a week. The vacuum pump even comes with reusable stoppers! You might think the decorative cork stoppers available on the market are cute to place on top of your open wine bottles but they don't *preserve* your wine. Use the decorative cork stoppers during parties, but remove them and employ some sort of a preservation system when the guests leave. To save your wine the same way many restaurants and bars do, Heels likes the Private Preserve®Wine Preserver. This canister inserts nitrogen into your wine bottle via a straw-like device. Nitrogen protects the wine from oxidation. Now, if you're alone and want to enjoy a glass of wine while reading a book, you won't have to worry having your wine go bad!

Corkscrews

Another tool you need to buy is a corkscrew. The only corkscrew worth investing in is a screw-pull corkscrew. It requires little to no muscle and makes the cork slide out in no time flat. It not only gives you a great wine image but is also a fun icebreaker for guests to use at parties. (Strictly for the use of corks!)

Other corkscrews cost much less. Some use two prongs to pry out the cork, and others screw into the cork counter-clockwise. Both can cause cork breakage. Symptoms that follow include bottlenecks breaking, not being able to get the cork out at all and naughty words. Take our advice. The screw-pull is one corkscrew you can't do without!

> **Sneakers and Heels Wine Tip:** The Rabbit™ brand screw-pull fits the Sneakers budget. Heels loves the Professional Screwpull® Lever Model since it comes with its own custom box and foil cutter.

Wine Glasses

Your image of wine is clearly reflected by the glass from which you serve it. Translation: Get rid of all your turquoise, gold-rimmed or hand-painted wine glasses. Colored or decorated wine glasses are a wine fashion "don't." Instead, use them for serving desserts. This statement might offend some of you, but a true wine-friendly glass needs to be clear and large-bowled. This is important because not only does it allow the drinker to clearly see, smell and taste the wine properly, but it also allows the wine to shine brightly.

We feel a Riedel crystal glass lets wine strut its stuff. These glasses are on the pricier side but are *so* worth it; even top chefs will agree! Think of them as your favorite pieces of jewelry. You can dress them up, sipping from it your fabulous library wine (a wine you've aged or saved for special occasions). You can dress them down to enhance an inexpensive wine. It's like having a choice between a Belgian chocolate truffle and a chocolate chip. The Riedel glasses are definitely the chocolate truffles; the glasses help accentuate a wine's essence and characteristics—allowing a wine's true personality to reveal itself. Experience some different wine varietal characteristics by trying the following: Buy a wine that's about $8. Pour a quarter of a glass into your pretty wine glass, and a quarter of a glass into a Riedel. Swirl them both around, and voilà! The wine will always taste better in the Riedel! You may have seen glasses designed for specific varietals. Don't feel the need to stock your cabinet full of these. Instead, buy Riedel's glasses designated for Zinfandel or Bordeaux wines, as these have the largest bowls. You can enjoy all wines from these beautiful glasses.

Tips for tasting wine:

- Only pour a quarter of a glass at a time. You can swirl like a pro without spilling over the sides.

- After you've poured the wine, place the glass on a hard surface. Hold the stem, keeping the bottom of the glass on the hard surface, and quickly draw an imaginary circle about the size of an orange. Do this about three times. This causes the wine to swirl around in the glass, releasing the wine's aroma and bouquet. Next, put your nose into the glass and take a long, deep whiff.

- Take a sip. Always drink your wine holding it by the stem, not the bowl. Holding your glass by the bowl causes the heat of your fingers to warm up the wine too quickly. Remember to think about the front, middle and finish of the sip. What is happening at each point?

- Hold the bowl of the glass when washing it. If you hold it by the stem, it'll snap in half! Been there, done that.

- Never put a Riedel glass in the dishwasher. Besides being too fragile, the detergent can leave a residue.

- Never wash under the influence (W.U.I.). Your chances of damaging your precious glasses would be greatly enhanced.

Crystal Washing Brushes

Riedel crystal wine glasses are like jewels to your wine. Keeping them, or any other glasses you choose, sparkling clean can be extremely challenging. The solution? Get yourself a crystal washing brush. They're specifically designed to clean crystal wine glasses without scratching, chipping or breaking them.

Stem Gems

These are your least expensive wine accessories. You can even make them yourself. Just pop into your local bead shop for lessons. Stem gems hook onto the stems of wine glasses to personalize your wine glass for the evening. Caution: Some people will forget what stem gem they had after a couple of glasses because: a) they were multi-tasking when choosing it or b) they were mad that someone already took the one they wanted. These people always end up with the gem they wanted, so protect your glass!

Wine and Food Websites

Internet wine and food websites are your instant links to wine and food recommendations, accessories, wineries and general wine information. All of the accessories mentioned above can be found on Internet wine and food websites. Use these websites as your personal home wine advisors—available twenty-four hours a day. It's all part of your continuing wine education. Some of our favorite websites include:

http://www.wineskinny.com
http://www.winespectator.com
http://www.localwineevents.com
http://www.caichef.edu
http://www.iwawine.com
http://www.wineenthusiast.com
http://www.costco.com
http://www.riedel.com

Worksheet
Other Useful Internet Wine and Food Sites

If you come across a favorite website, jot it down here.

Chapter 7-Cooking With Wine-Friendly Recipes

Do your dinners resemble a stale old black and white movie? Splice in some new colors; make them look and taste like blockbusters! Try these friendly wine and food fusions; they're quick to prepare and are guaranteed to lift and enhance palates. Look for other wine and food fusions in wine and food magazines, and Internet wine websites.

> **Sneakers and Heels Wine Tip:** If a wine is keeping its fruit under tight watch, like a young tannic red wine that needs a little more time to settle down, here is a little secret: try using a fruit-based sauce or marinade to lure the fruit back out of the wine. For example, raspberry mustard sauce poured over pork is terrific for luring the fruit out of a young Zinfandel or Syrah. In contrast, pear marmalade poured over chicken or white fish is a friendly fit for a Pinot Grigio or Sauvignon Blanc.

Berry Wine Sauce for Red Meat

This sauce can be made ahead of time and refrigerated. Just microwave it a couple of minutes before serving meat. It's perfect with Syrah, Zinfandel and Cabernet Sauvignon. (See substitution of fruit for Cabernet Sauvignon.)

- *1 8-ounce can blueberries*
- *1 8-ounce can raspberries (substitute cherries if serving Cabernet Sauvignon)*
- *½ cup red wine (preferably the one you'll be drinking)*
- *2 tablespoons red wine vinegar*
- *½ cup water*
- *3 tablespoons butter*
- *1 tablespoon sugar or to taste*

Puree berries in blender or with hand-held mixer. Place in a saucepan. (Make sure you have a large pan, or the berries will splatter out everywhere!) Add wine, red vinegar and water. Cook over medium heat, stirring occasionally, for approximately 30 minutes or until half the mixture has evaporated. Add the butter, one tablespoon at a time, and then the sugar. Serve warm with beef tenderloin or sliced porterhouse steak.

Wine Recommendation: Richard Partridge Cabernet Sauvignon

Super Fast but Elegant Halibut

- *2 pounds fresh halibut*
- *1 jar mango chutney*

In a hurry? Grab some fresh halibut (enough for your dinner party). Grill it or throw it in a pan, just long enough to brown the outsides. Toss in the oven for about 20 to 30 minutes. When done, pour a couple of tablespoons of warmed mango chutney over your fish and voila! Incredibly awesome!

Wine Recommendation: Montevina Pinot Grigio

Zinful Beef Tenderloins

- *¼ cup blackberry sage tea jam*
- *1 clove garlic*
- *2 cups plus 2 tablespoons red wine (preferably Zinfandel)*
- *2 tablespoons gourmet blue cheese*
- *Fresh ground pepper to taste*
- *1¼ pounds beef tenderloin*

The morning of your dinner, place the tenderloins in a bowl with 2 cups of red wine (saving the remaining 2 tablespoons for later), a clove of fresh pressed garlic, and ground pepper. Let marinate. Just before dinner, put jam in a small saucepan. Add the remaining 2 tablespoons of red wine and blue cheese; stir and heat slowly on low. While it's heating, grill the tenderloins. Just before serving, sprinkle blue cheese crumbs on top of the tenderloins. Pour sauce over the tenderloins and serve. (Fabulous for special occasions!)

Wine Recommendations: Marietta Old Vine Zinfandel (delectable) or Alexander Valley Estate Bottled Cabernet Sauvignon

Sneakers and Heels Wine Tip: Heels loves to serve dinner guests these Zinful Beef Tenderloins. The taste is exquisite when paired with Cabernet Sauvignon or Zinfandel!

Smoked Peach Poblano Chicken Pasta Salad

- *1 box bowtie pasta*
- *1 bunch green onions, chopped*
- *1 jicama, average-sized, peeled and chopped*
- *½ pound red grapes, chopped*
- *¼ cups pecans, chopped*
- *½ pound to 1 pound grilled chicken, cooled and diced*
- *1 jar smoked peach poblano salsa*

Boil pasta and drain. Mix all ingredients together in a large bowl. Toss with salad dressing (see recipe on next page) and between half and the entire jar of salsa, depending on your taste preference. Sprinkle fresh shredded Parmesan cheese on top. Don't forget to make copies of the recipe in advance. Your guests will request them at the end of the meal!

Smoked Peach Poblano Chicken Pasta Salad Dressing

- *1 cup Spin salad dressing (in the mayonnaise section)*
- *¼ cup milk*
- *1 clove pressed garlic*
- *1 tablespoon fresh lemon juice*
- *1 tablespoon fresh basil*
- *¼ cup fresh dill*

Mix all ingredients together. Gently toss through the pasta.
Wine Recommendation: Trinchero Sauvignon Blanc

C.T.'s Tender Topper Mushrooms

- *¼ pound Gorgonzola cheese chunks*
- *2 quarts fresh mushrooms*
- *¼ cup butter*
- *Clove fresh garlic*
- *2 tablespoons fresh chives*
- *¼ cup red wine*
- *2 tablespoons balsamic vinegar*
- *2-4 grilled beef tenderloins*

Sauté mushrooms and garlic in butter over medium heat for 10 minutes. Add red wine and balsamic vinegar. Simmer and cover for another 10 minutes. Remove from heat. Sprinkle Gorgonzola cheese chunks on top of grilled steak. Pour mushrooms over and on sides of steak. Sprinkle fresh chives for color.

Wine Recommendation: Chateau Potelle Old Vine Zinfandel Amador County

Red, White and Blue Brie Wheel

- *1 small wheel Brie, uncut*
- *1 quart fresh blueberries*
- *1 quart fresh raspberries*
- *1 jar mixed berry preserves*
- *1 mint leaf*

Slice the Brie wheel horizontally so it is sliced in half like a cake round. Lift the top off and spread mixed berry preserves on top of the bottom Brie round (like frosting the middle of a cake). Place the other Brie half on top of the other and spread the mixed berry preserves on top of it. Then, starting with the outer circle, place raspberries side by side in a circular pattern. Then, place blueberries side by side, circling the raspberries. Alternate fruits until top of the Brie is filled with raspberries and blueberries. Top with a mint leaf in the middle of the Brie. (Figure one small Brie wheel per four adults.)

Wine Recommendation: EOS Paso Robles Zinfandel

Sneakers and Heels Wine Tip: Sneakers loves to serve the Red, White and Blue Brie Wheel at book club gatherings.

Lily Pad Floats

- *¼ to ½ pound chilled Dubuque Roast Beef Slices**
- *1 pound cream cheese*
- *1 onion, chopped*
- *1 tablespoon garlic powder*
- *Fresh basil leaves*

Mix cream cheese, onion and garlic until creamy. Take one slice of roast beef at a time and spread it out flat. Spread mixture onto roast beef. Roll up slice and cut into about one-inch rolls. Pierce it with a toothpick to keep it together, and place each roll on a basil leaf. Continue until you have used all of the roast beef slices. *Turkey can be used in place of roast beef.

Give the illusion they're floating! Fill a large bowl with water. Add some food coloring and place plastic wrap tightly over the bowl of water. Place the Lily Pad Floats on top of the plastic wrap.

Wine Recommendation: Luna Di Luna Sangiovese/Merlot

Berry Zinful Quesadillas

- *1 package burrito-sized flour tortillas*
- *1 pound lean ground beef*
- *2 tablespoons balsamic vinegar*
- *¼ cup Zinfandel wine (preferably the wine recommendation below)*
- *4 tablespoons mild Gorgonzola or gourmet blue cheese*
- *2 tablespoons blackberry preserves*

Brown the ground beef. Pour the balsamic vinegar and Zinfandel wine into the browned ground beef. Let simmer 3-5 minutes on low to medium heat. Spoon the preserves and cook just long enough to warm up the mixture. Next, spray a non-stick griddle with cooking spray, and place a tortilla on it. Spoon approximately 6 tablespoons of ground beef mixture on half of the tortilla. Top with 1 tablespoon of cheese. Fold in half and let brown on bottom. Flip over to brown other side. Cut into six slices (pizza-style). Serve immediately. For an extra berry zinful taste, use a jar of hot pepper raspberry preserves as your salsa! (Makes approximately 4 quesadillas or 24 slices.)

Wine Recommendation: Cline California Zinfandel

Novel Wines Cheese Spread

- *½ teaspoon garlic flakes*
- *1 tablespoon onion flakes*
- *2 cups real mayonnaise*
- *½ pound each Colby, Swiss, and Velveeta*
- *1 teaspoon dry mustard*
- *1 tablespoon sugar*

Shred cheeses. Combine all ingredients. Refrigerate. Makes approximately four cups.

Wine Recommendation: Coppola Rosso

Fruity Angels

- *1 pint fresh raspberries*
- *1 pint fresh blueberries*
- *1 pint fresh blackberries*
- *½ cup blackberry liqueur*
- *2 oversized muffin pans*
- *1 box angel food cake mix*
- *1 jar hot fudge*
- *Fresh mint leaves*

A few hours ahead of time, put all fruit and liqueur into a bowl and let marinate in refrigerator three to four hours. Mix the cake according to directions. Pour into individual oversized muffin pans. Bake at 375 degrees for approximately 20-25 minutes or until crusty brown. Turn the muffin pans upside down to cool. (Hint: balance the pans over glass mixing bowls.) Once cool, use a serrated knife to cut off the tops of the cakes, making sure to cut evenly. Turn the cakes upside down and place on individual plates. Spoon fruit topping over the cakes and down around the sides. Place a mint leaf in the middle of each cake. Drizzle with hot fudge immediately before serving. (If you have any remaining cakes, freeze them!)

Wine Recommendation: Rancho Zabaco Dancing Bull Zinfandel

Worksheet
Your Wine Friendly Recipes

If you've changed a recipe and made it wine-friendly, record it here.

Chapter 8-Wine Image
Reviews to Use and Amuse

The following wine reviews take the characteristics of wine and bring them to life. Wines become people, animals or objects. It's an entertaining way to enjoy the art of wine and learn more about it in the process.

Check monthly for Sneakers and Heels personal wine recommendations on our website http://www.novelwines.com. Sit back, have a glass of wine and enjoy some Novel Wines images!

Kenwood Sauvignon Blanc Sonoma County 2000

The ocean kept calling to her as the heat became more unbearable. She peered over the railing of the private *oak* yacht, fingering her *floral* hairpiece before *pulling* it from her hair. She kicked off her heels, ripped off the *golden* sundress and plunged deep into the cool water, slowly resurfacing like a *lemon* yellow submarine.

Sail on your own private yacht with this wine. The oak is privately subdued; fingers of fruit and floral pull your palate in deeper. After it plunges you into its fruit, a lemon pops up to buoy the body.

Hint: Kill the heat of any spicy dish with this one!

Clients: This yacht's affordable, so sail on!

Friends: Buy a few cases! It's skinny-dipping time!

Price Category: Sneakers

Penfolds Rawson's Retreat Shiraz/Cabernet Sauvignon 2001

They were upgraded to Sir *Cherry's* Penthouse at no extra cost! The doors *opened* to the most *spectacular* suite she'd ever seen. *Dark cherry*-colored window treatments *seductively dressed* the *massive* windows. *Abstract* paintings of *red-stemmed* cherries adorned the walls. She flipped on the sound system. *Spicy* jazz wrapped its arms around all the rooms. Her *licorice* thin lips cracked a smile.

This wine is a penthouse at no extra charge! Its dark cherry fruits seduce your senses, before jazzing it up with some spice and licorice at the end. You can't help but smile at the price!

Hint: Buy a case or two! Pair with Brie topped with warm black cherries and a little jazz, please.

Clients: This is a no-brainer for the money!

Friends: My penthouse at 7:00! Be there!

Price Category: Sneakers

Montevina Sierra Foothills Zinfandel 1999

The *dark* bear stopped at the abandoned campsite and *shook* her head *to and fro,* trying to rouse the other bear. Her *nose kept focused* on the task at hand, and she continued *sure-footed* towards the smell that was luring her there. At last she found the grove of *blueberry* bushes! She gorged until her *large body* was full!

It takes a little air to wake up these large dark black "Bear-ries!" Once awake, the fruit is sure-footed until the very last drop!

Hint: Pair this with grilled chicken or pork, topped with raspberry crunch mustard! A "bear-y" good mix!

Clients: For your "not-so-heavy-duty" client.

Friends: See where their noses take them!!

Price Category: Sneakers

Domaine Serene Yamhill Cuvee Pinot Noir 1999

Her *fingers slid* through her *long silky* hair as she sat pushing the *oak* log *back* and *forth* with her feet. She popped the *ripe black cherries* into her mouth one by one. This moment of *complete indulgence* and inner peace was *rare*—she *lingered,* admiring the *perfect* view from the hill.

This silky Pinot Noir slides down smoothly with hints of oak rolling back and forth. Ripe black cherries keep popping in and out the all way down and then linger, just long enough for you to indulge in it some more.

Hint: Be at peace splurging on this one! Pair it with ham, salmon or even beef tenderloin.

Clients: For smooth operators only.

Friends: A magnificent choice for a night of complete indulgence!

Price Category: Heels

Turley California Old Vine Zinfandel 2000

The *dark, exotic* racer stretched out her *taut* muscles on the racetrack. *Jumping* back up to her toes, she *danced around, trying to shake out* her arms. Her *thick, muscular* legs dressed in *tight raspberry* leggings danced to another beat. She *lingered* around the *start* line before settling into her position—*short* of the *finish* line.

This dark Turley beauty is thick and muscular. The arm and leg muscles of the raspberry fruit are fighting one another as to who's going to loosen up first. The wine lingers quite awhile at the start, but finishes short. It needs more time in your cellar before it's completely limber.

Hint: If you run with this one, stretch out the fruit with red raspberries and blueberries; run it with Brie.

Clients: Turley trains only the best. Don't blow it on a non-contender.

Friends: This one will always draw a crowd!

Price Category: Heels

Richard Partridge Cabernet Sauvignon 1999

The queen hawk perched *elegantly* on the *oak* waiting for prey. Her binocular eyes spotted the *rare red* Mercedes turning onto *Blackberry* Mountain Road. Strong, rapid wing beats sailed her high into flight before she maternally *glided up* along side the car, almost protecting it through the *tightly* curved road. The driver softly exclaimed, "They'll have to witness *this one* in person!"

The elegant blackberry fruit rapidly sails the wine high. Once it opens up, the fruit glides along smoothly through the finish, leaving a lingering experience that all must witness!

Hint: This wine is a fabulous cellar selection! If you open it now, pair it with beef tenderloin medallions topped with warm berry compote or a touch of ground pepper.

Clients: Seal the phenomenal contract with this one!

Friends: Be protective and share only with rare wine friends!

Price Category: Heels

Worksheet
Create Your Own Wine Image Reviews

Get your creative juices flowing and write your own reviews. E-mail them to us!

Chapter 9-30 Wine Do's and Don'ts

If you're time-pressed, use this chapter as a quick wine refresher. Take a deep breath. Ready...set...read!

DO'S:

1. Do create your own personal wine contouring tasting kit and keep the necessary items on hand.

2. Do serve appetizers that need white and red wines to keep everyone happy. (Stay away from smoked salmon!)

3. Do figure six full glasses of wine per bottle—or one bottle per person!

4.   Do store your wines in a cool area of your house, away from any direct light.

5.   Do dress your wine and food alike. Heavier foods need heavier wines and vice versa.

6.   Do befriend a wine manager you can trust.

7.   Do stick with the simple rule of white meat, white wine and red meat, red wine.

8.   Do tell your server if your red wine is too warm.

9.   Do give wine as a gift. Red is best.

10.   Do only pour a quarter of a glass of wine at a time.

11.   Do use wine and food Internet websites.

12.   Do go to wine tastings to keep up your wine image.

13.   Do take this book with you when out shopping for wine.

14. Do think of wine and food pairing as nothing different than making a peanut butter and jelly sandwich.

15. Do match the color of your sauce or marinade to your wine.

DON'TS:

1. Don't forget to record what you ate with each wine and the wine label information in your Tasty Wine Encounters diary in the next chapter.

2. Don't expose your palate to any strong flavors such as toothpaste, mints or gum one hour prior to tasting any wine.

3. Don't ever buy wine because it has a pretty label.

4. Don't ever serve wine from a box or plastic glasses. You'll ruin your wine-savvy image!

5. Don't order your dinner wine until you've decided on a dinner entrée.

6. Don't hold any wine glass by its bowl. It's amateurish. Hold it by the stem.

7. Don't let your restaurant server intimidate you into ordering a wine immediately. Tell them you need a few minutes.

8. Don't forget to use your wine-buying ABCs. Always know why you're buying wine. Before you buy, know if you'll need a red or a white wine. Cost needs to be determined.

9. Don't forget to check the vintage on each bottle of wine you buy or order.

10. Don't forget to use the worksheets at the end of each chapter.

11. Don't forget to invest in wine accessories.

12. Don't buy decorative cork stoppers to preserve leftover wine. Use them instead as a fun conversation piece during parties. After the party, use a special wine preserver system to keep remaining wine from spoiling.

13. Don't shop at wine sales without your wine-buying formula.

14. Don't just serve any old food with wine. Use our wine-friendly recipes.

15. Don't forget—you're a wine chic woman!

Chapter 10-Tasty Wine Encounters

Continue learning about wines by recording every wine you drink until all of the following pages are filled. Some of your best wine education will come from these notes; this information is straight from the palate's mouth! Enter wines you liked as well as those you disliked. Follow this format and continue to review your entries. Were the wines you disliked from a mediocre vintage? Are the wines you always seem to love from a certain region? Be sure to look back and see how exquisite your wine face looks!

Wine Diary Tasty Encounter Notes
(Copy front of label, country, food served with wine, cost and place.)

Wine Diary Tasty Encounter Notes
(Copy down front of label, country, food served with the wine, cost and place.)

Wine Diary Tasty Encounter Notes
(Copy down front of label, country, food served with the wine, cost and place.)

Wine Diary Tasty Encounter Notes
(Copy down front of label, country, food served with the wine, cost and place.)

Wine Diary Tasty Encounter Notes
(Copy down front of label, country, food served with wine, cost
and place.)

Wine Diary Tasty Encounter Notes

(Copy down front of label, country, food served with the wine, cost and place.)

Wine Diary Tasty Encounter Notes
(Copy down front of label, country, food served with the wine, cost
and place.)

Wine Diary Tasty Encounter Notes

(Copy down front of label, country, food served with the wine, cost and place.)

Wine Diary Tasty Encounter Notes
(Copy down front of label, country, food served with the wine, cost
and place.)

Wine Diary Tasty Encounter Notes:
(Copy down front of label, country, food served with the wine, cost and place.)

Send Us Your Before and After Wine Makeover Stories

We'd love to hear from you! Send us your before and after wine makeover stories. Share with us your most embarrassing wine moments, or how this book has helped you with your wine dilemmas. With your permission, we might publish them in our next book! Be sure to tell us how we can contact you. Here's to you!

Send your stories or comments to the authors at:
Novel Wines Inc.
1630 Quail Ridge Circle
Woodbury, MN 55125
U.S.A.

Or e-mail us at:
novelwines@earthlink.net

Look for other *Wine Chic Women* books in the near future.

Give Wine Chic Women as a Gift

If you'd like to order additional copies of *Wine Chic Women* please go to   http://iUniverse.com,   http://barnesandnoble.com   or http://www.amazon.com

Or call iUniverse at:
1-877-288-4737